# SOLDIER'S HEART

*Tammy Ryan*

**BROADWAY PLAY PUBLISHING INC**
224 E 62nd St, NY, NY 10065
www.broadwayplaypub.com
info@broadwayplaypub.com

Cover artwork: Cassia Sakmar, Conservatory of Performing Arts, Point Park University

I S B N: 978-0-88145-670-7
First printing: July 2016

Book design: Marie Donovan
Word processing: Microsoft Word
Typographic controls: Xerox Ventura Publisher 2.0 P E
Typeface: Palatino
Printed and bound in the U S A

SOLDIER'S HEART received its world premiere at
The REP at the Pittsburgh Playhouse, the professional
theater company of Point Park University (Ronald
Allan-Lindblom, Artistic Producing Director), on 27
September 2013. The cast and creative contributors
were:

CASEY JOHNSON ................................Marie Elena O'Brien
MARGIE...............................................................Jenna Cole
CAPTAIN CHRISTOPHER BAINES .................. Michael Fuller
STAFF SERGEANT THOMAS WILLIAMS..... Justin Lonesome
LANCE CORPORAL JAMIE HERNANDEZ... Jaime Slavinsky
KEVIN....................................................Joshua Elijah Reese
SEAN .............................................................. Sundiata Rice

*Director*............................................................John Amplas
*Scenic design*.................................................Gianni Downs
*Lighting design* ..........................Andrew David Ostrowski
*Costume design*.............................Cathleen Crocker-Perry
*Video design*............................................ Jessi Sedon-Essad
*Stage manager*...................................................Caitlin Roper

SOLDIER'S HEART was next produced at Premiere Stages (New Jersey premiere), John Wooten, Producing Artistic Director, in the Zella Fry Theatre at Kean University on 10 July 2014. The cast and creative contributors were:

CASEY JOHNSON ................................................ Mairin Lee
MARGIE ........................................................... Kim Zimmer
CAPTAIN CHRISTOPHER BAINES ........ Michael Colby Jones
STAFF SGT THOMAS WILLIAMS .......... Landon G Woodson
LANCE CORPORAL JAMIE HERNANDEZ.... Erica Camarano
KEVIN ......................................................... Benton Greene
SEAN ............................................................. Azlan Landry
IRAQI BOY ................................................. Zane King Beers

*Director* ........................................................... John Wooten
*Dramaturg* ..................................................... Clare Drobot
*Scenic design* ............................................... Joseph Gourley
*Lighting design* .......................................... Nadine Charlsen
*Costume design* ................................................ Karen Hart
*Video design* ........................... Bryan Pekarek/Ian Alfano
*Stage Manager* ....................................... Dale Smallwood
*Casting director* ............................................ Carol Hanzel

# CHARACTERS & SETTING

*(Home)*

CASEY JOHNSON. *30 years old, Sergeant in the Marines, Assistant Commander of Convoy Security, Military Police.*

MARGIE, *58 years old,* CASEY's *mother. Former alcoholic, chain smoker, works at Foodland.*

KEVIN, *32, father of her son, ex-Marine, rides a Harley, works at Home Depot, African-American.*

SEAN,10, CASEY *and* KEVIN's *son, favors his father, wired like his mother.*

*(Iraq)*

STAFF SERGEANT THOMAS WILLIAMS, *early 30s,* CASEY's *immediate superior, African American, a good "by the book" Marine.*

LANCE CORPORAL JAMIE HERNANDEZ, *25 years old, East Coast, Latina, a gunner in* CASEY's *humvee.*

CAPTAIN CHRISTOPHER BAINES, *40,* CASEY's *Commanding Officer, a charmer, white.*


*Southwestern, Pennsylvania near Pittsburgh. And in Iraq.*

*The play begins in September 2006 and ends in June 2007.*

*After Fallujah, before the Surge.*

# NOTE ON SCENE CHANGES

The movement of the play should be fluid and transitions should happen quickly avoiding blackouts for costume changes. In the original production, Casey was dressed in her Marine fatigues that she dresses in for her deployment throughout, gradually shedding pieces of it as the play progresses. While in flashbacks others might be dressed for combat, Casey can be partially dressed and in her stocking feet. The scene design should facilitate changes between home and Iraq, but can also suggest a melding of the two, since Casey brings the war home with her. Sound design can help locate shifts in time and place. Cell phone video footage can be used where indicated in the script and in aiding transitions, but it is easy to overuse this device, rely on the instincts of a good video designer when you can. Less is more.

To First Sergeant Billy Jenkins, USMCR, with gratitude

# ACT ONE

## Scene One

*(At rise: MARGIE sits at the kitchen table, an unlit cigarette in her hand. She's drinking a cup of coffee. CASEY enters dressed in a white tee shirt and fatigues, her hair pulled back in a bun, and in her stocking feet. She carries a large box, the rest of her uniform draped over her arm and a metal box that she puts on the floor. She carefully drapes the clothes over a chair. Next to the box is a pair of combat boots.)*

MARGIE: It feels strange to be sitting at this kitchen table. You like living here?

CASEY: Sure. It's all right.

MARGIE: There's a reason that sonovabitch left the house to you and not to me.

CASEY: You hated each other, why would he leave the house to you.

MARGIE: You sure I couldn't take Sean back to my place? It might be more comfortable there.

CASEY: This is where he lives now, Mom. The less upheaval he has to go through the better.

MARGIE: Well, I feel like "He" doesn't want me here.

CASEY: Oh come on Mom. It's been almost six months. He's long gone. You don't believe in ghosts. Well, I don't.

MARGIE: What's in that box?

CASEY: *(Smiling)* Instructions.

MARGIE: I can take care of him without a manual. I raised you without one.

*(CASEY looks at MARGIE raising an eyebrow.)*

MARGIE: I raised you. On my own, and I didn't do that bad a job. Give me that at least, Casey. Your father gave you a house but not much else.

CASEY: *(Ignoring her comment, now referring to her box of "instructions")* Are you going to remember all of his doctor appointments? The dentist, the eye doctor, the dermatologist if his rash comes back, the drug store to call in his prescriptions? All the phone numbers you need are in here, plus his insurance card and vaccine record, and what he's allergic to—

MARGIE: I know he's allergic to penicillin. That's medical. I'll take all that.

CASEY: *(Pulling out bundle of large envelopes)* These are all of his afterschool activities. For each one you have to register him. I've filled out all the forms right here, and I made a calendar of when to sign him up for soccer and basketball and baseball starts this year too. You don't want to miss the registration because they fill up fast. And they won't take them ahead of time, I asked, so you'll have to do it. The checks are stapled to the forms. All you have to do is hand them in. On time.

MARGIE: You've always been an organizer.

CASEY: *(Pulling out another bundle)* This is all of his academic stuff. In fourth grade, he's going to have a lot of projects. He's responsible for knowing when things are due, but you have to know too, so you can make sure he remembers. I broke each one down here and also cross referenced on the main calendar.

MARGIE: Does it have to be so complicated?

CASEY: It's very simple. This is the master calendar. And then I have nine smaller ones broken down month by month. But if you think you can remember on your own…fine.

MARGIE: Okay, just give me everything.

CASEY: Then there's some personal stuff. Things I want you to talk to him about. Ask him every day, who he sat with at lunch, what they played at recess.

MARGIE: I don't need instructions for that.

CASEY: You've got to talk to him and keep him talking while I'm gone, he's not going to volunteer how he's feeling and he needs someone to talk to. You've got to pay attention, Mom. I don't want anybody bullying him at recess and if you find out something is going on, call Kevin.

MARGIE: You baby that kid. Let him fight his own battles.

CASEY: Not while I'm not here. Somebody's got to have his back. Promise me.

MARGIE: Okay.

CASEY: I want him reading chapter books this year. So take him to the library one Saturday a month. That's on the master calendar. Limit the D S, T V , and computer. Mom, listen to me, no more than one hour of screens a day.

MARGIE: He can't watch a movie.

CASEY: Hire a babysitter if you need one, there's a list of names to call. Or call Kevin. Kevin's got him every other weekend, so you'll have a break then. Really Mom, I'm gonna be gone for nine months, he can't be sitting around playing those games for nine—

MARGIE: Okay, okay, one hour of T V and one hour on the computer.

CASEY: That's two hours. If he sits in front of a screen all day long he's gonna get constipated and cranky and then he doesn't want to do anything, it's a downward spiral. He needs to stay active, get him outside to run around.

MARGIE: Is he going to have time for that, with all of his other "activities?"

CASEY: *(Unruffled)* Mom, you promised you'd do this my way. *(Returning to her list)* Okay, encourage him, praise the effort when he's working hard, but don't say good job for every little thing he does.

MARGIE: I do know something about what kids need. No matter what you think: I raised you—I did—and look at you. Look what you've made of your life. Look how you're handling all this. I'm amazed by you, Casey.

CASEY: Don't be amazed by me. I'm just doing what needs to be done.

MARGIE: What's in this little box?

CASEY: A digital recorder. Sean knows how to use it. Each track has a recording of me reading one of his favorite stories. He can just push a button and listen to the one he wants, before he goes to bed. There are also letters on here—and if you don't mind they're private. Every one ends with me saying I love you. But, I want you to say it to him too. He needs to hear it out loud. I know you're not a big hugger, but a hug at night, every night. Please?

MARGIE: I never thought I'd be in this position, saying goodbye to my daughter going off to war.

CASEY: *(We agreed)* No tears, Mom.

MARGIE: You don't seem scared! You don't even seem worried!

CASEY: I've got a job to do over there, and that's what I intend to do. Besides, I'm looking forward to it. If it weren't for Seanie I wouldn't have any reservations about going.

MARGIE: But what about the danger, Casey, what I been reading about in the papers? What about those I U Ds?

CASEY: I E Ds. They got people to take care of them. And I'll be on the bases, mostly. Which are very protected areas.

MARGIE: You keep saying that. But I don't see how you're not going to have to be on the highways some of the time, if all you do is go base to base, you're going to have to go through-—

CASEY: Mom.

(MARGIE *stops.* CASEY *packs up the box.*)

CASEY: I'll be on the base most of the time. And the other times, well, that's why I'm going there: to provide security.

MARGIE: Your father would be peeing himself, he'd be so proud.

CASEY: I bet he'd be a lot of things. Proud is not one that comes to mind. *(She ties her boot laces tight and quick.)*

MARGIE: Oh no, Casey honey, he was proud. He left you this house didn't he? He was always proud you went into the military. Not that he had that much to do with it.

CASEY: We never talked about it.

MARGIE: You outrank him. That was not lost on him. And now you're going into a war zone….he couldn't lord it over you with his war, no more…because now…you'll have your own—war.

(CASEY *picks up the metal box.*)

MARGIE: What is that?

CASEY: His gun from Vietnam. I found it when I was going through some of his crap out in the garage. It was in a duffle bag. Bullets right next to it.

MARGIE: So what do you want me to do with it?

CASEY: Bring it to your place. Put it in the attic or somewhere. I don't want it around when I'm not here.

MARGIE: I don't want it.

CASEY: It's locked. Here are the keys. Just put it away somewhere.

MARGIE: I don't care, Casey, I do not want that in my house. I don't even want to touch it.

CASEY: (*Checking the time, moving towards the closet with the metal box*) It's ten to already—I gotta get Sean. I'm putting it in the closet, on the top shelf, all the way in the back. I'm taking the keys with me. (*She puts the keys on the dog chain around her neck, then returns to the table, crossing the next item off her list.*) One last thing.

MARGIE: You've always been a planner. Since you were a little girl. I've never planned a thing in my life. No surprise there.

CASEY: This letter. Keep it aside. Sean doesn't read this. Unless. You know. Something happens. If something happens.

(MARGIE *looks clueless at the letter.*)

CASEY: I don't come back.

(MARGIE *takes the letter. She starts to tear up as she turns away, putting the letter in her bag.*)

CASEY: (*Quickly now, time is running out*) I want you to take him to church. Doesn't have to be every single Sunday but enough that the priest knows his name—

MARGIE: *(Stops crying/overlapping)* …Oh my God…

CASEY: Do you want to help me or not? He needs to go to church.

MARGIE: Okay, okay, church too. Every…other Sunday.

CASEY: If any of this is confusing, or if you have a question just shoot me an email.

MARGIE: Will you be able to check your email from there?

CASEY: I should be able to most every day I'm at the base. Sean knows he can email me whenever he needs to. And we can skype too.

MARGIE: Skipe? I hope he knows how to do that.

CASEY: He does.

MARGIE: What?

CASEY: One final request. And I know this will be hard for you. But please don't smoke in the house. Sean's asthma. Really, don't do it. It stinks up the place. It took me six months to get the smell out of these walls. Seriously.

MARGIE: Okay, okay. I'll go home and smoke. I'm going to have to go back to my house sometimes, you know, to get some things. I'm not moving in here. *(Beat)* I'll smoke outside.

CASEY: I've got to go. I want to be there when school lets out. We're going to get pizza then I'll bring him back. The more matter of fact we can be, the better off he'll be.

*(MARGIE nods. CASEY puts on her cap and exits. MARGIE sits with the box alone for a moment fingering her cigarette. She wants to smoke. She looks around the room as if her ex husband is going to pop out of a cabinet. She opens the box, picks up the bundles of severely organized envelopes, an expression of being overwhelmed crosses her face. She picks*

*up the digital recorder, looks at it without a clue how to make it work. Pushes a button:)*

CASEY: *(Voice over, singing)* "I see the moon and the moon sees me, shining through the leaves of the old oak tree, oh let the light that shines on me, shine on the one I love—"

*(CASEY returns, standing behind MARGIE, watching her for a moment, then singing the last line with the recording. MARGIE jumps, stops the recorder.)*

MARGIE: Jezus Mother of God. You scared the living crap out of me! What? What is it?

CASEY: In case I forget later. *(She hugs MARGIE.)* I know we've had our differences. But I love you, Mom. For real. Always have. Always will.

MARGIE: Thank you for telling me that. I love you too, baby.

CASEY: Okay, let's not get carried away. Make sure you put those back in order.

*(CASEY winks at MARGIE who stands there fighting back the tears, unable to say anything there is so much to say.)*

CASEY: I'll be back in one hour with Sean. No Long Goodbyes.

*(MARGIE nods. CASEY smiles reassuringly, exits. MARGIE picks up the envelopes, checking the labels to get them in order. She picks up the digital recorder about to put it away when she pushes the button. We hear CASEY's voice continue to softly sing the rest of the lullaby as the lights fade slowly as MARGIE listens.)*

CASEY: "…over the mountains, over the sea, back where my heart is longing to be be, oh let the light that shines on me, shine on the one I love…" *(Speaking softly)* Sleep tight, Buddy. Mama loves you. Be home soon.…

*(Lights shift.)*

## Scene Two

*(Nine months later. Four o'clock in the afternoon)*
*(CASEY stands in the middle of the room, dressed in her combat fatigues as before. She's changed considerably in terms of her physicality and her affect, she's lost weight, is physically tight, she clears her throat repeatedly. She drops her duffle bag. MARGIE comes in after her, fussing around, talking nonstop to fill the empty air/space/vacuum, that CASEY's presence yet absence creates.)*

MARGIE: …So I picked up a few things after work I thought you might like, but we can do a big shopping at Foodland later once you and Sean get settled and know more what you'll need. You'll need milk, and bread that's for sure. That boy eats a lot of bread by the way. I can't believe how much that boy eats. Then he wonders why he gets a stomachache. He's so excited to see you, Casey, I was going to bring him to the airport, but Kevin said you were—well.

*(During the above, CASEY reflexively checks the perimeter of the room, including the ceiling, under the table, into the other rooms, offstage, returning quickly. She stops, facing MARGIE who stands in front of the closet.)*

CASEY: *(Interrupting her mother, mid stream)* Excuse me.

MARGIE: What?

CASEY: Open it.

MARGIE: Nothing but coats in there.

CASEY: I said open it. Since you're standing in front of it. Or move, so I can open it.

MARGIE: Okay. *(She steps aside.)*

CASEY: Thank you.

MARGIE: Want me…to make coffee?

(CASEY *doesn't answer as she looks into the closet, moving coats so she can see down the length of it, moving her hand along the shelf. Satisfied, she closes the door.*)

MARGIE: Do you want some coffee, honey?

(CASEY *takes out some hand sanitizer, squirts some into her hands, rubs them together quickly, a tic she will repeat.*)

CASEY: I gotta take a piss.

(CASEY *exits to the bathroom.* MARGIE *is a little taken aback, but continues to talk: a running stream.*)

MARGIE: Maybe I won't make any. I've had about a pot already. I was so nervous waiting for your flight. I was worried I don't know why, that you wouldn't be on it! Thank God you're home, that's all I can say. I worried about you the whole time you were over there, thank god you're all right. Thank God you're in one piece. We are all so happy you're home. Sean's gonna be so happy. We are all so proud of you.

CASEY: No.

MARGIE: What do you mean, no, of course we are.

(*As* MARGIE *talks* CASEY *gets up, looks out the window. More hand sanitizer*)

MARGIE: I even have a button on my smock at work, says Proud Mom of a Marine. People come to my register, see my button, and say, oh, is that your son in Iraq and I say, no, my daughter. And Sean's so proud, he can't wait to tell you, he did a report about you at school—for one of his projects this year—wait until you see how tall he got—

CASEY: I said, no, Mom.

MARGIE: What? No, what? No Sean? Don't be ridiculous.

CASEY: I'm not going to see him.

MARGIE: What do you mean not going to see him?

CASEY: ...Not now.

MARGIE: Casey. Your little boy has waited nine months for you to come home. I honored your wishes by not bringing him to the airport, and it broke my heart to see his little face, when I told him he couldn't come. I don't understand this. We were expecting a reunion. Tears hugs, smiles. This is—this is—I don't know what this is—

CASEY: Get on your cell and tell Kevin to turn around. Now. Or I'm walking out the door.

MARGIE: Casey, hon, you don't mean that.

CASEY: Let Kevin keep him for a while. He's his Dad.

MARGIE: That man can't keep a pair of goldfish alive. I'm not saying he's not a good man, he was a big help, that's for sure, but he's not gonna be able to take care of Sean full time. Who's gonna watch him when he's at work? With that boy's asthma—

CASEY: What about his asthma?

MARGIE: Oh, one time Kevin took him out somewhere and I guess he forgot to take his inhaler. We ended up in the hospital that night. I emailed you about that. Look, he did the best he could—we both did.

CASEY: You didn't burn the goddamn house down. I'll give you credit for that.

MARGIE: I never smoked in here.

CASEY: (Picking up MARGIE's ashtray and dumping it in the trash) You're a bad liar.

MARGIE: Well, maybe I smoked a one here and there, when it was freezing cold outside, when we had all that snow, but I opened the window, and I never ever

smoked in front of him. I did the best I could Casey
honey, but that little boy needs his Mom.

CASEY: His mom is not here. Tell him that—tell him I
missed the plane. I don't care what you tell him.

MARGIE: He knows you're here. I just told you. He's on
his way over here with Kevin right now.

CASEY: Take out your cell. Call Kevin right now and
tell him to turn around. Goddamn do it.

(MARGIE *takes out cell phone.*)

MARGIE: Okay, you don't have to talk to me that way—

CASEY: *(Overlapping)* Obviously I do.

MARGIE: *(Overlapping)* I took care of that boy for nine
months, now I'm not looking for a medal—

CASEY: Get on the Mother Fucking Phone!

*(As* MARGIE *dials,* CASEY *exits briefly towards bedrooms.)*

MARGIE: Jezus Christ. Your language, honey, you never
talked to me like— Hello. Kevin. Its Margie. Yes, we're
here. Today…might not be a good day. She's not—no.
No, no just tell him. You tell him she's not—.

*(He has handed Sean the phone)*

MARGIE: Seanie. Yes, she is. Listen honey. Your mother
is not up for a visit today. I know hon, I know and you
will soon. She's just— tired from her long plane trip.
She's jet lagged, you know how when you travel across
time zones you get real tired. Your biological clock gets
all turned around. It's going to take some time for her
to get back to this time period. She loves you. She loves
you, she says, she loves you and she'll see you real
soon. She's gotta…get a little sleep first. Tomorrow,
first thing I'm sure. Tell your Dad, I'll be over to pick
you up in a little while and then we'll go to my house
and watch a movie tonight, how's that sound? Put
your father back on the phone, put your father—.

*(He's hung up.)*

*(CASEY hands MARGIE a child's backpack.)*

CASEY: Don't be bringing him over here tomorrow. Kevin can come for the rest of his stuff later.

*(Long pause. MARGIE faces CASEY completely at a loss. Abruptly, MARGIE picks up her purse, finds her keys. Picks up a few more things that belong to Sean, some clothes out of a basket on the kitchen table, etc. and shoves them into the backpack.)*

MARGIE: I'm not asking you to tell me what the hell happened to you over there believe me, I went through this with your father and to be honest I don't want to know. But you are not the daughter I sent over there.

CASEY: Thank you for all you did, Mom. *(Beat)* I really want to be alone now.

*(MARGIE stares at CASEY a brief moment, exits. CASEY does not move from the spot. She stares straight ahead vacantly. Silence. CASEY moves to the closet and finds a large box, rummages around until she finds a bottle of Tequila, her Dad's stash. She takes a swig then stares at the box of instructions sitting in the closet, unopened. Next to the box is the digital recorder. She picks it up and stares at it for a moment, then pockets it. She reaches up towards the top shelf and pulls out the locked metal box returning with it to the table.)*

*(Behind her, CAPTAIN CHRISTOPHER BAINES, emerges from the hall closet. She reacts as if he is in the room with her.)*

BAINES: You sure you want to open up that Pandora's box?

*(CASEY reaches for her dog chain, the keys are not there, lost. She pulls a knife from a drawer and gets to work on the locked box.)*

BAINES: Once you open it, you can't close it again, Sergeant.

(CASEY *pops open the box, pulls out the gun.*)

BAINES: What good do you think is gonna come of that?

(CASEY *presses the gun under her chin.*)

BAINES: That's not a good choice, Sergeant.

(CASEY *tries to pull the trigger, but doesn't.* BAINES *pushes the bottle of tequila a little closer. Then he exits back into the closet.* CASEY *lowers her weapon. Lights shift.*)

## Scene Three

*(Desert. On the side of MOBILE, the main supply road between Al Asad and everywhere else in Iraq, heading north. The sun is setting, the sky is orange.* STAFF SERGEANT WILLIAMS *approaches* CASEY*)*

WILLIAMS: We keep moving, Sergeant. That means we don't stop. When we are rolling through Indian country we don't stop. I don't care if it's a man a woman a camel donkey or dog, you keep this convoy moving that's your job. If little Haji's on the side of the road waving at you, it's not the motherfuckin Macy's Day parade, he's getting ready to launch a goddamn rocket in your lap.

CASEY: Kellerman thought he saw something, so he slowed—

WILLIAMS: Stop right there. Kellerman was driving? Kellerman's in the gun.

CASEY: Hernandez told me she's a gunner. Staff Sergeant.

WILLIAMS: Kellerman's the gun. Hernandez drives.
You're on the radio and Martins is fuckin useless keep
him in the back.

CASEY: Hernandez is a better gunner than Kellerman in
my opinion.

WILLIAMS: Your opinion, based on what, Sergeant
Johnson. The ten minutes you been here? Hernandez
drives.

CASEY: Hernandez told me she's a gunner. And she
pays attention. Unlike Kellerman.

WILLIAMS: That's an order, Sergeant. *(Half a beat)* Back
there in the market, when that local and his goats were
blocking the road, you got out of the Humvee.

CASEY: I was moving him along, Staff Sergeant.

WILLIAMS: You send out Martins. He can do that.

CASEY: It was easier for me to just—

WILLIAMS: What did I just fuckin say? *(He waits a beat.)*
A crowd was gathering, looking at you like Pocha-
fuckin-hontas. I had a decision to make back there.
I don't want to find myself in that position again,
Sergeant.

CASEY: What decision? Nothing happened, they
dispersed.

WILLIAMS: A female marine is not going to get herself
gang raped by a crowd of locals on my watch. If
somebody made a move, I would've had to take you
out, Sergeant.

CASEY: I don't need you to make that decision for me.
Staff Sergeant.

WILLIAMS: I'm sure you're competent. Hernandez
is a shining star, but you both make my job more
complicated. Like right now: you're trying to figure
out where you're gonna take a piss. I can't be worrying

about pitchin a goddamn tent on the side of MOBILE
so you ladies got privacy. This is the last pit stop til
Tikrit—six hours from now. You got thirty seconds
to take care of your business, Sergeant. You hold me
up today, I got Captain Baines up my ass, and if he's
up my ass, I'm not happy. If I'm not happy, nobody's
happy. Lance Corporal, explain Standard Ops to her.

(WILLIAMS *exits.* HERNANDEZ *has her back to* CASEY *and
is pissing at the side of the road like a man. She is younger
than* CASEY, *but this is her second deployment, and she's
been in this unit longer. She glances at* CASEY *who's looking
around for somewhere discreet to squat down.*)

HERNANDEZ: If you're not gonna grow some balls,
Sergeant, you better carry a dick in your pocket.

CASEY: Excuse me? How—are you doing that?

HERNANDEZ: Made it. Out of spare parts. Got tired
of looking around for a bush to pee behind out in the
middle of nowhere.

(HERNANDEZ *takes the device out of her pants, shakes it off,
and shoves it in a pocket.*)

HERNANDEZ: If you're not gonna grow any in the near
future, you'd better make yourself one. Here. *(She
throws her the hand sanitizer.)* You wanna be careful
about hygiene. You don't want a UTI out here, believe
me. Some advice, Sergeant: drink as little as humanly
possible. But don't get dehydrated. You want to sweat;
you don't want to pee.

CASEY: You're driving, Lance Corporal.

HERNANDEZ: I heard. *(Referring to* WILLIAMS*)* His bark's
worse than his bite. But he's right, Sergeant: you don't
want Captain Baines up his ass—or yours.

CASEY: Baines seems decent. Williams has been all over
my shit the minute I got here.

HERNANDEZ: You plugged a hole in this unit, Sergeant. You're replacing someone who was well liked. You're never gonna measure up. *(A small smile)* You miss your little boy.

CASEY: I know it hasn't been that long.

HERNANDEZ: Don't make friends with the locals. They smile at your face, but they're givin ya the finger behind your back or rockin you from an overpass. You gotta watch out when they're on an overpass.

CASEY: That boy in the market was harmless.

HERNANDEZ: How old do you think he was?

CASEY: Eight or nine.

HERNANDEZ: If they look eight, they're closer to thirteen. They're runnin around barefoot on blacktop in hundred twenty degrees. They're not normal kids. Put your little boy out of your head while you're here. Put him in a little box and lock him up, till you get back home. That's what I do.

CASEY: Do you have a son?

HERNANDEZ: *(Doesn't answer her question)* Did you get the shots? So you don't get your period?

CASEY: No, I didn't.

HERNANDEZ: You may wanna do that. They don't call it being on the rag out here for nothing. *(Starts to exit)*

CASEY: Hernandez, wait.

HERNANDEZ: There's no bush to squat behind in the sandbox, Sergeant. *(Pulls out an empty water bottle that has been cut in half)* S O P.

*(CASEY looks blankly.)*

HERNANDEZ: You piss in it. Back in the Humvee, Sergeant.

(HERNANDEZ *exits. Lights shift as sound of Humvees roaring down the desert highway.*)

## Scene Four

(*The sound of the Humvee transforms into the sound of a door bell buzzing. Lights up.* MARGIE *faces* CASEY.)

MARGIE: Weren't you going to answer the door?

CASEY: I answered it.

MARGIE: Took you long enough. What'd they feed you over there? You're nothing but skin and bones. You were always skinny, but look at you. You got no ass, Casey.

CASEY: Uhm. Thanks.

MARGIE: Are you eating? Want me to make you a sandwich?

CASEY: What do you want, Mom?

MARGIE: It's been a week now. I came to see how you're doing. (*Pause*) So, how are you doing?

CASEY: Do you have aspirin or anything?

(MARGIE *digs in her purse.*)

MARGIE: Aren't they helping you?

CASEY: Who?

MARGIE: Who else? The people who sent you over there. The people who said they were gonna take care of you when they signed you up straight out of high school. Or the ones who said join the Reserves when you get out, just on the weekends, while you're going back to school. Then they call you back to go to war. Them. What are they doing for you? They gotta at least help you transition.

CASEY: No.

MARGIE: Well, I'm sorry I'm having trouble believing that. What's the V A for then?

CASEY: Fuck if I know.

MARGIE: Your father was always going to the V A.

CASEY: There was a lot wrong with him.

MARGIE: Isn't there something wrong with you to be acting this way?

CASEY: Oh, there's plenty wrong with me. But their solutions for what's wrong with me aren't good ones.

MARGIE: But what if they can help you?

CASEY: They won't! I already talked to some of those assholes. They're not gonna help me Mom. Besides I don't want to drive. So I have no way of getting up there. So forget it.

MARGIE: I could drive you. I have off Mondays and Fridays. I can take you.

CASEY: I got a headache and I gotta take a piss. Maybe you better go.

MARGIE: Don't shut me out, Casey. It's not good to be alone like this. Let me help you.

CASEY: A fuckin aspirin would help.

MARGIE: *(Digging in her purse)* I got some ibruprofen in my bag. Here, keep the bottle. I can get some more at work.

*(CASEY swallows a few then chases it with Tequila.)*

MARGIE: Casey, what the hell's wrong with you! You're supposed to take that with water, not tequila. What the hell are you doing? You want to turn into your father, drinking his beverage of choice? You want to go down his path?

CASEY: Or yours?

MARGIE: *(After a beat)* I don't deserve that. I'm not saying I didn't drink too much, but you can't compare me to your father. He came back from Vietnam and was drunk every day since, and abusive on top of it. You can't say that about me.

CASEY: Bring him to Kevin's.

MARGIE: That's not the answer.

CASEY: If he's too much for you, bring him to his father's.

MARGIE: I had him for nine months, Casey. He's an active boy.

CASEY: So then give him to Kevin. Or sell him on ebay! What are you talking to me for? I'm giving up custody. I don't want him in this house. I'm unfit. My head is pounding.

MARGIE: You're his mother.

*(CASEY doesn't answer. Instead we hear the sounds of a cell phone video, children shouting, laughter. In the corner a shadow of A BOY standing in the doorway of the closet.)*

CASEY: Call foster care. You did it before.

*(MARGIE stares at CASEY. Exits. After a moment, sound of a rifle shot. Lights shift.)*

## Scene Five

*(As lights rise she faces CAPTAIN BAINES who sits in a chair behind a small metal desk.)*

BAINES: I told Williams he's gotta stop smokin that crack pipe, but either he's still smokin that shit… or…you're just hard to get along with. Which is it, Sergeant?

CASEY: I try to get along with everyone, sir.

BAINES: Relax, Marine, I'm making a joke. At ease, Sergeant. I'm not here to chew you out. I just wanted some face time with you. That's all. Sit.

(CASEY *sits across from* BAINES.)

BAINES: How do you like the Sandbox so far?

CASEY: I'm adjusting, sir.

BAINES: That's a good way to put it. Adjustment is an ongoing mission here, I'd say. Flexibility will take you far, Johnson.

CASEY: Yes, sir.

BAINES: You just need some time to learn our system. I want you to fit in, Sergeant. Unit cohesion is my number one. I hear you don't eat with the other marines.

CASEY: We've been doing back to back convoys, sir. I haven't had time. We get back late, I just fall into my rack. Besides, I'm a vegetarian, there's not a lot for me to eat.

BAINES: How come every female they send me is a vegetarian? We offer vegetarian choices. I don't know what they keep alive besides a squirrel. You might have to break that vegetarian habit, get some meat on your bones. You're a little scrawny thing, aren't you?

CASEY: I beg your pardon, sir?

BAINES: You got any problems with anybody in this unit, you come straight to me. Unit cohesion is my number one. I'll take care of you.

CASEY: I appreciate that, sir.

BAINES: That includes Williams. Sometimes I question that boy's leadership abilities. Don't be afraid to come to me.

CASEY: I'm not questioning his abilities, Captain.

BAINES: Heard you have a little boy at home.

CASEY: Yes, sir.

BAINES: What's his name?

CASEY: Sean.

BAINES: How old is Sean?

CASEY: He'll be turning ten, sir, in a few months.

BAINES: Who's taking care of Sean while you're here?

CASEY: My Mom, sir.

BAINES: Sean's father not in the picture?

CASEY: He is, but, we're not married, sir. We work together, though, to do what's best for him.

BAINES: I like to hear that. Put the kid's interest first, right? That's good. He serve? Your ex?

CASEY: Two tours. He's out now, sir.

BAINES: Deployments are tough on relationships. I know; I'm divorced myself. No kids, though. I sympathize with you, Sergeant, it is not easy to have to leave your little boy at home and go and serve your country.

CASEY: We're a military family, so he knows what to expect. He'll be all right, sir.

BAINES: I'll speak to Williams, but I don't think I've got a problem here, Marine. You say your father was in the military.

CASEY: Army. Vietnam. He passed six months ago.

BAINES: I'm sorry to hear that. You're carrying a lot your plate, aren't you?

CASEY: Nothing I can't handle, sir.

BAINES: Tough cookie. Hell, you're a marine. All of us in the Marines, men and women. We're all Marines first. But we're also all only human. You know what

I'm saying. Anybody bothers you, anybody gives you
any kind of problem you come straight to me. I've got
zero tolerance for any of that nonsense. Seriously. You
come straight to me. Think of me as your Daddy in the
Desert.

CASEY: Excuse me, sir?

BAINES: Sense of humor, check, Sergeant. I'm making a
joke. Wouldn't hurt you to smile.
When you get to know me better, you'll see, I like to
make light of a situation, when I can. It relieves stress.
Seriously. We can all use a little stress relief, around
here. Am I right? *(Beat)* Like I said, we all get along in
this unit. I want us to get along.

*(BAINES stands, CASEY stands. A moment)*

BAINES: Here.

CASEY: What's this for, sir?

BAINES: My sat phone. Keep it. In case you need to call
home. Direct.

CASEY: Thank you, sir.

BAINES: All right.

*(CASEY stands. Lights shift.)*

## Scene Six

*(In the darkness, the door bell. Then knocking. Then louder
knocking. Lights rise on the empty livingroom/kitchen. A
pause in the knocking, then a key in the door is heard.)*

*(The door opens and KEVIN enters. He is clearly ex military,
strongly built with a quiet centered demeanor. He's dressed
in a motorcycle jacket and jeans. He is holding his helmet;
his hair is cut close.)*

*(As* KEVIN *enters, he scans the perimeter of the room, much as* CASEY *did earlier, heading towards the rooms offstage. He looks into them, quickly returns to the couch, snapping off the blanket.)*

KEVIN: Where the hell is she?

*(At that moment* CASEY *pops out from the cabinet under sink pointing her weapon at* KEVIN. *[Note: in a less realistically designed set,* CASEY *can pop out of anywhere—a door/behind couch, etc. But she should NOT come out of the closet, The closet is* BAINES *domain.* CASEY *would not go in there.])*

*(*KEVIN *reacts immediately, stepping back, behind the couch, arms raised.* CASEY *lowers her weapon as soon as sees him.)*

KEVIN: Whoa! What the fuck are you doing in there?

CASEY: What the fuck are you breaking into my house for?

KEVIN: I walked in the front door! Your Mom gave me the key! *(Referring to the gun)* Somebody gonna miss that at the base armory?

CASEY: No. It's mine.

KEVIN: It better be, Sergeant.

CASEY: It is, don't worry.

KEVIN: Since when are you Annie Oakley?

CASEY: Little present from Dad. Some girls get sports cars. I get a haunted house and a loaded weapon.

KEVIN: Doesn't seem like you.

CASEY: People change. I bet you have one.

KEVIN: Put that away and keep it locked up. I don't want to see that again. You camping out here? *(He moves around the room, his hand on his chest to calm his hammering heart, as he checks out evidence of the way* CASEY's *been living.)*

CASEY: Little jumpy, are we?

KEVIN: What do you think? You pop out like a jack in the box. I never liked those things, even when I was a kid. Never saw the point of a toy that gave you a heart attack. *(Beat)* You sleeping on the couch?

CASEY: If I remember correctly, you slept on the floor when you got back.

KEVIN: I'm not judging, just an observation.

CASEY: I keep hearing noises, just easier to be out here.

KEVIN: You gonna stay under there?

CASEY: Maybe.

KEVIN: Casey, come out of the there, I can't talk to you hiding in there.

CASEY: I can't.

KEVIN: Why can't you?

CASEY: Woke up with vertigo. Every time I move the world starts spinning. I haven't gotten off the couch all day. Till you started with all that banging.

KEVIN: I rang the doorbell first. You didn't answer.

CASEY: Maybe I didn't want company.

KEVIN: How'd you get from the couch to there if you can't stand up?

*(CASEY falls over and starts crawling.)*

KEVIN: Here, I can't watch that, let me help you up.

*(KEVIN takes CASEY's arm, lifts her up and drapes her over his shoulder, carrying her to the couch.)*

CASEY: Don't touch me! No, Kevin! NOhhhh, the room is spinning...put me the fuck down!

KEVIN: *(Overlapping)* Easy, easy, easy. You're okay. Hey. *(He lays her down on the sofa then throws a blanket over her, backs off a little, looking at her.)*

CASEY: If I'm very still and don't move my head, it stops. Sort of.

KEVIN: Maybe you need to get that looked at.

CASEY: I'm fine.

KEVIN: Maybe you should go see a doctor.

CASEY: Why, so some Psycho-Terrorist can tell me it's all in my head.

KEVIN: It might be a sign of something serious. They might be able to give you something for it. *(Pause, then referring to her weight loss)* Looks like the food's still gourmet over there.

CASEY: Food sucked.

KEVIN: I don't miss that, I tell ya what.

CASEY: Was there something you missed?

KEVIN: You know what I miss? The simplicity. Only two things you need to do over there: one, the mission, two, stay alive. Here I got a gazillion and one things to do every day and that's before I go to work. I swear I don't know how people don't lose their minds on a daily basis.

CASEY: Who says they don't.

KEVIN: Truth.

CASEY: When you went for your second tour, I couldn't understand why in God's green earth you would do that. But I get it now.

KEVIN: You do, huh? Well that's something.

CASEY: All I wanted to do was come home. Every single minute I was over there sucked. But still I keep thinking about certain things. Like at night. It's so eerie and dark and you're sitting there waiting to get shot at, then a rocket goes off in the distance, and you think, goddamn, that's beautiful. Meanwhile some bastard just got blown up in his field.

KEVIN: The difference between a massacre and the 4th of July is just your Position on the Ground.

*(Pause)*

CASEY: I felt safer there. I know that makes no sense. But that's how I feel.

KEVIN: It's like one looong Christmas eve when you're over there. All you do is talk about what you're gonna do when you get back, who you're gonna see, what you're gonna eat, how much you're gonna party. Then you come back and it's like one big fuckin hangover. And Santa forgot to come to your house. *(Brief pause)* Speakin of Santa not comin to your house. We got one disappointed little boy on our hands.

CASEY: Take him Kevin. Please just take him. I raised him the first ten years you take the second. I'm not capable. I'm not—his mother anymore.

KEVIN: *(Impatient)* You're always gonna be his mother.

CASEY: I can't sleep, I can't eat, I gotta take a piss every frigging half hour, I can't even stand up! And I don't know if I—I don't trust myself around him. He's better off with you.

KEVIN: Uh-huh. *(He paces a bit, restless, shaking his head.)* Fine. He can stay with me. We're having a good time.

CASEY: That was too easy.

KEVIN: I know you, Cakes, you're an Indian giver. You'll change your mind and want him back just when we're getting comfortable. It's temporary.

CASEY: I'm glad the two of you are having so much fun, but I'm not changing my mind.

KEVIN: It's not always gonna feel like this. It's never gonna go back to the way it was, but it will get somewhat more bearable. Trust me.

CASEY: Really? I didn't notice that when you got home. I thought you were pretty unbearable, from beginning to end—

| CASEY: *(Overlapping)* | KEVIN:*(Overlapping)* |
|---|---|
| —throwing shit, flippin out on Seanie, frickin nightmares… | Water under the bridge, Cakes. Water under the bridge. |

CASEY: So it was okay for you to be the way you were but because I'm his mother I better get my shit together?

KEVIN: I know it was no picnic for you over there. Shit sure hit the fan after Fallujah. So, no, it's not going to be easy re-adjusting. I know that. Believe me. I was rocked, shot at, blown up, bombed and almost set on fire and still I think about going back. The thing that stops me now is Seanie.

CASEY: Were you raped?

*(KEVIN stops talking.)*

KEVIN: Say again?

CASEY: Oh sorry. Not raped. Military Sexual Traumatized. That's what they call it.

KEVIN: Did you report that shit?

CASEY: What do you think?

KEVIN: You need to report this, Sergeant!

CASEY: To who?

KEVIN: You know who. You go to your chain of command.

CASEY: Right. And then what?

KEVIN: Then they investigate.

CASEY: Then they arrest me for fraternization, conduct unbecoming, or adultery. Even though I'm not married. You know the drill. I'm not the first woman got raped in the military.

KEVIN: *(Pause)* Who was it?

CASEY: You don't know jack shit about being a woman in the Marines.

*(Silence for a beat while KEVIN absorbs this.)*

KEVIN: Goddamn it. Who was it, Casey. Don't go radio silent on me now.

*(CASEY doesn't answer.)*

KEVIN: All right. Even if you take all your earned leave, you only got about twenty-six days before you gotta report back to duty. You look to me like you're gonna need more than that. Go to the V A, tell them whatever you want, but get your benefits while you can.

CASEY: There you go with that double standard bullshit again.

KEVIN: No shame in asking for help. If you need it.

CASEY: I don't need it! I'm home, I'm alive. I survived that shit! Fuck them. I'm not their victim. And fuck you. I don't need the fuckin V A.

KEVIN: You can't get up off the couch.

CASEY: I'm working on it. That's the vertigo. It's gonna pass. Don't look at me like that. You didn't go to the V A. When your contract was over, and you were acting like a fucking maniac, I asked you to go, and you didn't go.

KEVIN: I wasn't raped.

CASEY: I shouldn't have told you.

*(Long pause as KEVIN takes her in.)*

KEVIN: Was this someone you were in a relationship with?

CASEY: You did not just fucking say that to me.

KEVIN: What? I'm not making judgments. I'm just trying to get the lay of the land. That was some load of shit you just dropped on me, Casey! Hey, I'm not implying anything, it's just I don't know what you been up to the last year, year and a half do I?

CASEY: *(Overlapping: an argument, neither one is listening to the other)* It's none of your business either way, asshole. That's a—that's a fucked up thing to say. One thing doesn't have anything to do with the other. It just proves my damn point.

KEVIN: *(Overlapping)* I didn't mean to offend. I apologize, okay? I'm—I'm just trying to help you.

CASEY: Forget it. You can't help me.

KEVIN: *(After a pause)* You know how if you scrape your knee on the road—

CASEY: *(Overlapping)* Oh yeah, that's what it's like—!

KEVIN: —All that gravel and shit gets worked in there. You get home. You don't wash it out. You just throw a bandaid on it. Then you forget about it, and you never take off that bandaid. What's gonna happen? It's gonna get red and sore and swell up full of pus. You gotta take off the bandaid if you want to clean out the infection. Maybe you gotta rip it off. Yes. It's gonna hurt. But it's the only way it's gonna heal. If you want to save your leg.

CASEY: Mister Analogy. Why don't you go back to fucking college and be a writer? You can make up all kinds of shit then, doesn't have to have anything to do with reality.

ACT ONE                                    31

KEVIN: I just might do that. Even with you mocking me. I just might. But that's not gonna help you is it?

CASEY: I'm fine.

KEVIN: *(Another pause)* All right. I got Seanie. For the time being. You work on getting off the couch. *(He takes his helmet and stops by the door. He looks at her a long time.)* I'm sorry that happened to you, Cakes.

CASEY: Lock the door behind you.

*(KEVIN nods, then exits. CASEY reaches for the tequilla.)*

*(Lights shift.)*


## Scene Seven

*(CASEY talks to Sean via skype from the desert. We don't hear his responses, which are few. She starts quickly, cheerful.)*

CASEY: One month down. It's gonna go fast. You got school, soccer starting, then basketball. I'll be back in time for soft—. Hey, it's temporary, Bud. I need to be here, you know that. I made a commitment. We can't back away from it now just because it's hard. *(Stops)* Gramma told me what those kids said. Their parents are not in the military. They don't know what they're talking about. We're helpin these people. You should see the kids here, honey, be glad you're safe and fed and taken care of—because it's not like that for everybody. I'll tell Dad to talk to your teachers—. Okay, then you gotta get tough, Sean. If those punks sense weakness, it's like blood in the water. That's how bullies work. It won't stop until you stop it. You gotta show them you're not weak.

*(The Skype starts to break up.)*

CASEY: Be strong, Sean. I'll be home…soon. I love you.

*(As the video breaks up it is replaced by cell phone video of Iraqi kids shouting and acting out for the camera. We see smiles, hands reaching out. It starts off friendly, but then gets louder, angry. Words shouted, like "Candy!" Give me dollars!" A boy's face breaks into a great big grin. The camera is shaky but we can hear his voice: "Madonna! Madonna! I love you! Madonna!" We hear a female voice off camera ask, "What's your name?" Response from the boy: "S'aheed!" "Tell me your name?" S'aheed!)*

*(Lights shift.)*

## Scene Eight

*(Lights bump up. CASEY is on the couch playing a video game, drinking from the tequila. MARGIE barges in, clearly pissed off.)*

MARGIE: He's got a baseball game today. I'm here to pick up his cleats and his glove. Kevin said they'd be in his closet, in his room.

*(MARGIE waits for a response from CASEY, doesn't get one)*

MARGIE: I'll just go and get them. *(As she walks past her into the other room)* Did you eat anything today? I brought you a sandwich.

*(CASEY doesn't respond, just keeps playing the game. MARGIE reenters with the uniform and cleats.)*

MARGIE: Okay where else could the glove be? It's not in there.

*(CASEY doesn't answer. MARGIE begins looking for the glove.)*

MARGIE: You're not gonna talk to me now. You're gonna sit there and drink your life away. That what you want to do? This isn't you, Casey, hon. Sitting here playing video games night and day. I don't know what's going on with you anymore, but this can't go on like this.

(CASEY *doesn't answer, keeps playing.*)

MARGIE: You're a rock head, just like your father. That's who I feel like I'm talking to. Where are you getting this liquor from? You don't leave the house. Is someone bringing this to you?

CASEY: Daddy had a stash. You know how alcoholics do.

MARGIE: You know what I keep thinking about? I keep thinking about the girl who left here at eighteen years old to go on that motorcycle trip with that boy from school, I don't remember his name, what was his name?

CASEY: Doesn't matter.

MARGIE: For weeks you were walking around the house making plans, looking at maps, all grown up. As if you were going someplace. In my mind I thought she won't do it, she'll get scared, she'll change her mind. She's not riding on a motorcycle across the country with that boy. Then that day you walked into my bedroom looking for something in my dresser drawer and I said, "You don't think I'm going to let you go do you?" And you looked at me in that resentful way you had and said, "You can't stop me. Tomorrow I'm walking out that door getting on that motorcycle and riding into the sunset." (*She finds the glove under the couch.*)

CASEY: That's not what I said.

MARGIE: What did you say, then?

CASEY: I said I may not come back.

MARGIE: That's right. You weren't coming back. And that's when it hit me. I was done. My job was done,

and you were going to live your life the way you
wanted to no matter what I had to say about it. Here,
eat this sandwich. Give me that. Stop playing that
game. *(She puts a sandwich in front of her.)*
*(CASEY ignores it and continues staring at the T V, playing
the game. MARGIE starts cleaning up some of the mess.)*

MARGIE: Here you were just barely eighteen years
old going across the country I had no idea where you
would be sleeping that night. And you were totally
confident. You had no doubt you could do whatever
you wanted. You were free and I was jealous it
wasn't me going on that motorcycle riding into the
sunset, if you want to know the truth. I never been to
California. I never saw the Rocky Mountains or the
Grand Canyon, or any of the places around the world
you were going to go to. Then you tell me you're
joining the military when you got back. Now I didn't
think that was a good idea then and in hindsight it
still doesn't look good. *(Pause)* Its summertime, Casey.
That boy needs something to do besides ride his
bike up and down the street. There are no kids in my
neighborhood. And after his game tonight, baseball's
over. What's he supposed to do all summer? *(Beat)*
What the hell happened to you over there?

CASEY: You don't want to know, Mom. That's what
you said.

MARGIE: Kevin didn't come back like this.

CASEY: You have no fuckin idea how Kevin came back.
You didn't live with him.

MARGIE: Whatever happened, whatever you saw
or experienced or did, I'm telling you right now,
I'd've gone over there for you. If there was anyway, I
would've been the one to go to Iraq.

CASEY: That makes no sense.

MARGIE: What you're doing: drinkin your life away, sitting in front of this X-Station, breakin your son's heart—this makes no damn sense. And this video game is the kid's and I'm takin it back with me right now so he can have a little enjoyment after his championship game and I'm gonna let him stay up all night and play it for hours!

*(MARGIE grabs the Xbox, taking the game with all the wires and equipment and tries stuffing it in her bag. CASEY yanks it all back.)*

CASEY: Don't fucking touch it.

MARGIE: Don't you care he's having his last game tonight? Do you know how it would light up his heart if you came to that game today?

CASEY: I can't get up off the couch, Mom. I can't walk to the door. I can't step outside without feeling like I'm gonna have a heart attack.

MARGIE: Listen to me, I'm gonna keep saying this over and over until you listen. Don't screw up your relationship with Sean. You can't get that back. Out of all the mistakes you're gonna make in your life, you're gonna regret that the most. That much I do know.

*(CASEY closes her eyes, arms over her head.)*

MARGIE: It's time to call the V A. Casey. I know you don't want to, but we have to. There are doctors there who can help you. Kevin told me. Psychologists and what not, you know, experts with helping people who went through what you went through. You were in a war, Casey, people don't always bounce back from that on their own. They sent you over there, now they have an obligation to help you! Let them help you!

CASEY: Fuckin Kevin should stay the fuck out of my fuckin life.

MARGIE: You know you don't give that man credit. He's on your side, Casey.

CASEY: What else did he tell you? Did he tell you— *(She stops, then starts up the game again.)*

MARGIE: There's a period of adjustment, and I understand that, but that for some people with Post something S T D whatever, it's harder. He said they got treatment for that. And there's no shame in it, Casey—Casey!

*(CASEY finally stops playing.)*

CASEY: I was raped. Did he tell you that?

*(MARGIE is finally speechless.)*

MARGIE: No. He did not tell me that—oh, sweetie—?

CASEY: Don't.

MARGIE: Oh my God, honey, baby. Who—were you captured, what happened??

CASEY: Fuck no. Captured. No. It was somebody in my unit. A superior. So I'm double fucked.

MARGIE: How can that be…? Did you tell anybody?

CASEY: You know what they call us Women Marines? Walking Mattresses. There's nobody to tell.

MARGIE: I knew the military wasn't a good place for a woman. I will kill that motherfucker.

CASEY: You can't touch him. You don't even know him.

MARGIE: I'm not talking about that bastard. I'm talking about the bastard that signed you up a year out of high school. The promises he made, "Don't you worry we're gonna take care of your little girl for you." Right. This is how you take care of her. *(Long pause)* What can I do?

CASEY: Leave me alone.

MARGIE: I don't feel right doing that.

CASEY: It didn't happen yesterday. I've dealt with it, all right. It was my own damn fault for getting myself in that situation.

MARGIE: No.

CASEY: There were no witnesses, Mom. It's his word against mine. He's judge, jury and executioner.

MARGIE: There's gotta be somebody else you can go to.

CASEY: Chain of command.

MARGIE: Well, I don't know what that means.

CASEY: It means there's nothing I can do except forget it. Look, Mom, I'm dizzy and these fuckin headaches and I gotta piss constantly and I don't trust myself around Sean anymore.

MARGIE: But you're his mother! It might help you to be his mother again.

CASEY: No. Why can't anybody hear what I'm saying? No, no, no. When I was in Iraq, I put him in a little box and lost the key. I don't have the patience, I don't have—I don't have any love for him anymore. He's somebody else's problem now.

MARGIE: That's not true—

CASEY: Hey, you bailed out on me. When you were drinking so much I had to step over you lying on the floor. Remember that? I need you to step up now. I need you to figure out something long term for him. Open up that letter I gave you and give it to him because his mother is fucking gone. She's gone and she ain't coming back. You gotta prepare him.

(MARGIE *hesitates.*)

CASEY: Go. He's waiting for his glove.

(MARGIE *exits. Lights alter. We hear sounds of the video game return, distorted with the sounds of the cell phone*

*video, then stop abruptly as* BAINES *steps out of the closet.*
CASEY *is immediately back in Iraq:)*

BAINES: Time for you and me to have a little heart to heart. You want to believe that we are over here doing the right thing. Get over it. War is not religion, it's not a noble "calling".

CASEY: It's a job.

BAINES: 'At's right. And your job is to do what?

CASEY: My job is to protect my marines.

BAINES: Your job is to follow orders.

CASEY: Yes, sir.

BAINES: Smile. That's an order. There you go. You look like a different person when you smile. You light up, you really do, like a flower in the desert. You should smile more often.

CASEY: No.

BAINES: You know what? I might have a little crush on you.

*(CASEY is silent.)*

BAINES: All right. Now I'm here to help you, Marine. That's my job. You can make my job easier, or you can make it harder.

*(CASEY doesn't answer.)*

BAINES: I sense tension. Do we need some stress relief, Sergeant? I'm gonna tell you a joke. That okay? That okay with you? Answer me!

CASEY: Okay.

BAINES: Okay, what?

CASEY: Okay, sir.

BAINES: Okay, Sergeant. What's the difference between...a slut and a bitch?

(CASEY *knows this joke.*)

BAINES: Come on what's the difference? Take a guess. What's a slut do? She sleeps with everybody right? And what about a bitch?

CASEY: She sleeps with everybody but you.

BAINES: 'At's right. See, you know it. So? Which one are you? My guess is…a bitch. The jury might still be out on that one. It's a choice you get to make.

CASEY: I want to be clear, sir. I don't do that.

BAINES: Do what, Sergeant?

CASEY: I'm not here for that.

BAINES: And that's why you've been flirting with me.

CASEY: Excuse me sir, I have not been—

BAINES: You don't find me attractive?

CASEY: You're my superior, sir. That's not appropriate for me to say—

BAINES: I asked you a direct question. Do you or don't you find me attractive?

CASEY: I—I—don't know, sir.

BAINES: I'm trying to help you here, Sergeant. In case you didn't notice, there's nowhere to hide in the desert. You need somebody to have your back. You can be a bitch if you want. But if you're my bitch, then everybody else will leave you alone. It's your choice.

(*The video game sound, the cell phone sound/images, and war noise, has begun to blend together in a rising dark static. THE BOY emerges from the shadows of the kitchen. We clearly see a child standing there, though his face remains obscured. CASEY reaches out for the bottle of ibuprofen. She takes a handful, then another handful until she swallows the whole bottle.*)

BAINES: That's not a good choice, Sergeant.

(CASEY *reaches out her hand for the bottle of tequilla. As
she drinks from it,* BAINES *retreats to his hiding place in the
closet.* CASEY *picks up the digital recorder and hits Play.
We hear her pre recorded voice talking to Sean. She listens
for a moment...*)

CASEY: *(Recorded)* ...freedom, buddy, is the most
important thing. We're fighting the bad guys so those
kids can have freedom, just like the freedoms you
enjoy—

(*Then* CASEY *hits the erase button. We hear the sound of
that tape erasing. She hits another button, and for a second,
we hear her voice reading a story.* THE BOY *is moving
towards her...*)

CASEY: *(Recorded)* —and climbed into the window and
into his room and she picked up that grown up man
and rocked him in her arms saying I'll love you for-—

(CASEY *hits the button. We hear the track erase. She hits
another button and we hear her voice, singing. The* BOY
*stands next to her, then crouches down...*)

CASEY: *(Recorded)* ...over the mountains, over the sea,
back where my heart is longing to be—

(CASEY *hits erase. We hear the sound of the empty track
playing.* THE BOY, *a long dark shadow sits next to her. As
his head falls slowly onto her shoulder,* CASEY *stares out.
Lights fade.*)

## END OF ACT ONE

# ACT TWO

## Scene Nine

*(Lights rise on the empty living room. Sounds of violent retching in the bathroom offstage. We hear calm comforting sounds coming from* KEVIN, *"that's right get it out, get it all out, just let it come out, breathe." After a moment, quiet.* KEVIN *enters with* CASEY *helping her back to the couch, who shakes him off, then wobbles back towards the couch, moaning.)*

KEVIN: I'm calling an ambulance.

CASEY: NOOOOO.

KEVIN: It was a half assed attempt, but it was an attempt. It's time, Casey. I'll strap you to my bike if I have to, but I think an ambulance is the better way to go.

CASEY: I shouldn'tve called you.

KEVIN: You should have called me and good thing you did. And now I'm callin an ambulance.

*(*CASEY *takes the gun from under the cushion, and points it at* KEVIN. *He reacts immediately: first with presence, then voice, then force.)*

KEVIN: What do you think you're doing? Put down your weapon, Sergeant.

CASEY: I'll shoot your fucking balls off, Kevin! I'm not going anywhere.

(KEVIN *disarms* CASEY *easily, takes out the clip, pockets both, then gets back to his cell phone.*)

CASEY: NO!

KEVIN: You're getting your stomach pumped.

CASEY: There's nothin left in there. It all came out. Gimme back my weapon.

KEVIN: Not a snowball's chance in hell—

CASEY: Please don't call them, Kevin, please, I can't go in an ambulance. Take me if you want. But just just give me a minute. Look I'm not dying. I'm fine, I'm just sick as a dog. Give it back. I'm defenseless.

KEVIN: Exactly. (*He looks at her a moment. Pause*) That's the second time you pointed this at me. I don't wait for three strikes, Marine.

CASEY: Oh come on, if I was gonna shoot you, I would have. I was just making a point!

KEVIN: So am I. What are you doing, keeping it under the cushions? What if Sean finds it?

CASEY: He's not here. Okay. Really Kevin, I need that pistol, to be able to breathe, I'm not fucking kidding.

KEVIN: Nope. (*He takes Gatorade out of the paper bag sitting on the table, cracks it open for her.*) Rest your stomach for half an hour. Then take small sips. If you keep that down, try soup.

CASEY: Fuck soup. I want my gun. Motherfucker.

KEVIN: Yeah. I guess you're gonna be all right.

CASEY: Don't go.

KEVIN: You're lucky, you know that.

CASEY: He's gone when you're here.

KEVIN: Who?

CASEY: Please stay. If you're gonna take my weapon, you gotta stay…jus' till I fall asleep. Please, Kevin.

KEVIN: 'Kay.

CASEY: Hold my hand?

(KEVIN *hesitates a moment, then takes her hand.*)

KEVIN: Roger.

(CASEY *softens, after a moment, leaning in to him.*)

CASEY: Don't tell my mother.

KEVIN: Unless she asks me point blank, "Did Casey try to off herself this afternoon?" I won't offer any information.

CASEY: Don't be telling her I need to go to the V A.

KEVIN: Well, you know how I feel. Only you know how you feel.

CASEY: …I feel sick…

KEVIN: Really? You just washed down a bottle of Motrim with a half a bottle of tequila, and I don't see evidence of food anywhere. You're lucky you don't have liver failure. You're not supposed to mix that shit.

CASEY: Wasn't a whole bottle. Not even half.

KEVIN: Still not good for your liver.

CASEY: Nothin wrong with my liver, it's my heart. It's dead.

KEVIN: It's not dead. It's just…frozen. Like those snowballs—you know you make 'em in the wintertime…

(CASEY *groans at the start of another analogy, but* KEVIN *soldiers on.*)

KEVIN: …and throw 'em in the back of the freezer, so you can have 'em come summertime. When it comes out it's hard as a rock, even harder then when you first

put it in there, cause it solidifies. But what happens
when you put that ice ball on the counter? Even that
hard as rock solid piece of ice is eventually gonna thaw
out.

CASEY: I'm never…

KEVIN: Hey, even glaciers melt in time.

CASEY: What about you 'nalogy man…you ever thaw
out?

(KEVIN *gives a small laugh.* CASEY's *right.*)

KEVIN: Hey, I like analogies. And I'll tell you why: you
can hold onto them. Not like military speak. There's
a reason they use acronyms instead of words. Like
a fistful of sand, they're meant to slip through your
fingers. M R Es. Right? Meal Ready To Eat, sounds
delicious. They are neither Meals Nor Ready. But
without the letters they gotta call it what it is: cold shit
in a bag you heat up till it tastes like hot shit in a bag.
Me, I like to hold onto what I'm saying. Even if I'm
only talking to myself. Which is what I'm doing most
of the time…. (*After a beat, answering her question*) Give
or take a thousand years…we might both thaw out.

(*Pause between* CASEY *and* KEVIN.)

KEVIN: Besides, as I remember it, you used to like my
analogies.

CASEY: Two and a half billion analogies later. (*Beat*)
Not everything is always like something else.

KEVIN: Maybe not.

CASEY: (*Then after a beat, quietly*) …Sean?

KEVIN: He's tough. Like his Mama.

(CASEY *is quiet, her throat constricts, but no tears.* KEVIN
*watches her.*)

KEVIN: Number one rule for a female marine, Never Let Them See You Cry.

CASEY: Semper Fi.

KEVIN: Semper Fi. Now that I still believe in. Nobody had your back out there in the desert. But I do. Always will.

CASEY: Except when we broke up.

KEVIN: I do know a little of what you're going through, Cakes. Now the shoe's on the other foot, huh? Maybe I can see what it was like for you...when I came back.

CASEY: You...been seeing anybody?

KEVIN: Nah. *(Another beat)* Hey. Even if we couldn't live with each other, I'm always gonna be there for you. And Sean. As much as I can be. *(Pause)* It's okay to shed some tears.

CASEY: I would if I could. A phantom leg is stuck in my throat.

KEVIN: I know how much you love Sean. How it tore you up to leave him that long. I know, I went twice. Finally, I said I can't do it anymore. Workin at Home Depot, helping little old ladies pick out faucets and garden hoses. I don't find that too thrilling. But I do it for him, so I can be around. I didn't have that growin up. And I want him to. I try to keep it no more complicated than that. *(Beat)* I also know this: he's gonna be all right. And so are you.

CASEY: If you're not gonna give me back my weapon, shoot me with it and put me out of my misery.

KEVIN: You still got a sense of humor in there. That's the life boat. Hold on to that. I know how it gets. That dull empty feeling. Boredom growing like a rope so thick I could strangle somebody with it. So maybe I drive my bike a little too fast down the highway,

passing on the solid, until I see some trash on the
side of the road. Then my heart starts beating about
a hundred and fifty miles an hour. Right? Because
a part of me stayed there, with my buddies in Iraq.
Wondering if they're keeping their heads down, maybe
I should be there with them. But I push through until
the end of another day… because what else am I gonna
do?

(KEVIN *stops himself. He stands up, shakes it off, balls up
paper bag, throws it out.* CASEY *watches.*)

CASEY: I didn't have any buddies in Iraq. So I don't
know what the hell you're talking about.

KEVIN: It's not easy. That's all I'm saying.

CASEY: I think I might sleep now. If I could stay here on
the couch.

(KEVIN *looks at* CASEY *for a moment.*)

KEVIN: Okay. I won't make you go to the hospital
today.

CASEY: That was too easy.

KEVIN: Yes, it was.

CASEY: You want something.

KEVIN: Yes, I do.

CASEY: You want me to go to the V A.

KEVIN: Believe me, I don't think they're gonna solve
all your problem, Cakes, but it's a start. It's you taking
action, instead of hiding away in here.

CASEY: Okay. Two conditions.

KEVIN: Go ahead.

CASEY: I'm not tellin them jackshit.

KEVIN: Fair enough. What's two?

CASEY: I need my weapon, Kevin. I need it. By the end I
had to take my rifle with me everywhere: to mess hall,
the showers, the head. I couldn't trust anybody. It's the
only thing that gets me from one minute to the next.
I'm not gonna use it. I give you my word. You can keep
the bullets. No, I need the bullets, too. Please, Kevin. If
you care about me at all anymore. If I was gonna use
it on myself, don't you think I would have already,
instead of making myself throw up with a handful of
friggin aspirin? I need it. It's like—like Sean's blanket.
'Member when we tried to take that away from him?

KEVIN: Sean's blanket, huh?

CASEY: I wouldn't take your bike, man. I wouldn't do
that to you.

KEVIN: *(After a considered pause)* Make the appointment
for a Wednesday or Thursday. My days off.

*(KEVIN hands CASEY the gun. Her hand closes on it. He
holds onto it before releasing.)*

KEVIN: Don't make me regret this, Cakes.

*(CASEY holds out her other hand. KEVIN reaches into his
pocket, drops the clip into her open palm.)*

*(Sound transforms into rifle shots as lights shift.)*

### Scene Ten

*(HERNANDEZ and WILLIAMS are looking through a case of
Meals Ready to Eat. CASEY looks defensive.)*

HERNANDEZ: Look at this. What am I supposed to eat?
The whole case has been ratfucked. All the crackers
and peanut butter is gone from every single one of
these. Who here is a vegetarian?

CASEY: I hope you're not implying that it was me who
ratfucked that case, Lance Corporal.

HERNANDEZ: There's no vegetarian option in this case, Sergeant. That's all I'm saying. And I can't eat this other crap. It makes me sick. And every single one of these has been opened and ratfucked.

WILLIAMS: I got two females, and two vegetarians so I'm twice ratfucked here so don't talk to me about your problems.

CASEY: I never touched them, Staff Sergeant.

WILLIAMS: I don't wanna hear this shit. Here, chicken, eat the goddamned chicken.

HERNANDEZ: They even took the fuckin milkshakes.

CASEY: I got a real problem with your attitude, Lance Corporal—

(HERNANDEZ *exits without saying another word.*)

CASEY: Did you see what she just did? She's been given me nothing but disrespect since I got here. What is her problem?

WILLIAMS: I suggest you eat one of these too. Here MRE 22, chicken and dumplings. I actually like that one. It's not bad.

CASEY: I want you to back me up with her. When I got here, I thought great, another female, maybe we could be friends, then I thought okay, maybe she's got to warm up to me, but she's cold as ice. And I did nothing wrong.

WILLIAMS: First of all, she's under you, she's not gonna be your friend, Sergeant.

CASEY: Okay, I'm not asking for friendship, but how about respect?

WILLIAMS: I don't know what to tell you. She's under your command, Sergeant. Are you telling me you can't handle her?

CASEY: I can handle her, I'm not saying that, but it doesn't have to be this way.

WILLIAMS: Before you got here, she was the only female. Maybe she sees you as the competition.

CASEY: Competition for what, I'm her superior.

WILLIAMS: There are rumors going around.

CASEY: What rumors?

WILLIAMS: Baines. She used to be his favorite, till you got here.

*(A brief stunned pause)*

CASEY: She can have him! I've got no interest in him! He's the one won't leave me alone. In fact, he's crossed the line more than once. Not only do I gotta put up with his bullshit, I gotta put up with hers? Does everybody think..? No, everybody here is looking the other way. You see what's going on. I know you do. You're not blind.

WILLIAMS: Are you filing charges against Captain Baines, Sergeant?

CASEY: Yeah and if I did I can kiss my career goodbye.

WILLIAMS: My advice is I don't have any advice.

CASEY: Well that's fucked up.

WILLIAMS: Excuse me, Sergeant.

CASEY: No excuse me, Staff Sergeant. You were gonna put a bullet in my head my first day in this unit, because you thought some of the locals were looking at me cross-eyed. Now this fucking guy, I'm sorry, my C O is getting ready to do something, and you won't even acknowledge that it's happening. *(Beat)* It's not safe for me here, Staff Sergeant Williams. So why don't you take me out now? How's it any different?

WILLIAMS: This is why women don't belong in this operation. That's my opinion. No one wants to listen to me.

CASEY: Yeah, well no one wants to talk to me. All of you are freezing me out, through no fault of my own. This guy's got it in for me because I won't come back to base between missions and suck his dick. I didn't go lookin for this. And I don't even have another female in this unit to be on my side. I don't feel safe walking to the damn showers.

WILLIAMS: Here's my advice. Take your rifle with you to the showers and shut up about it. You made your choice when you signed up. What did you think when you joined the corps—did you think it was gonna be a tea party? Male and Females thrown together and no sexual tension? Who did you think was gonna be here with you? They're fuckin boys missin their girlfriends. With hard ons for you the minute they laid eyes on you, not because you're all that, but because you're a woman. Excuse me, female. Like that makes any difference to their dicks. *(Beat)* You got two choices. You can go along. Or you can make waves. If you make waves, you're not gonna be makin friends. Period. You can't have it both ways. Doesn't work that way. *(He takes the Chicken with Dumplings, and exits.)*

*(Lights shift.)*

## Scene Eleven

*(HERNANDEZ sits on CASEY's couch, where CASEY is usually parked. CASEY stands in the middle of the room.)*

HERNANDEZ: I can't remember how to work the T V. My husband got a big flat screen while I was gone, and it's got three different remotes. One for the T V, one for the cable, another one for the D V D player, one turns it on, one switches to the H D, another one works the channels. I'm sitting there, totally confused, I don't know what to do, finally my daughter grabs the remote from my hand, one two three, she's watchin Dora the Explorer. Kids, right?

CASEY: Right.

HERNANDEZ: My little girl just started kindergarten. Yeah. She's doing real good now. Took her some time to adjust to me being back. My husband spoiled her rotten while I was gone. But that's okay, if you can't spoil them now while they're young, right? That's what my therapist tells me. *(Pause, hesitates, but asks)* How's your little boy?

CASEY: Ever notice how the word Therapist, sounds a lot like Terrorist?

HERNANDEZ: Must be using up your earned leave by now. You going for your benefits?

CASEY: I don't know what I'm going to do.

HERNANDEZ: I haven't been able to sleep since I got back and I'm real short with my daughter. She had no idea why her mother's such a bitch, right? I just see something in her eyes I don't like when she looks at me, and I decide I better talk to somebody.

CASEY: What are you doing here, Hernandez?

HERNANDEZ: Have you been to the V A?

CASEY: I tried to get something for my headaches. They left me on hold.

HERNANDEZ: Me too. But I kept trying till I got my appointment and I went. So they give me all these forms to fill out and the guy there says "I only got time for one today. Check which symptom you want to be seen for. " So I say: M S T. *(Beat)* And he goes M S T, oh wow. Really? Okay, I wish you hadn't said that. But

here you go, like twenty more forms I gotta fill out.
Including this narrative, they want me to write.

CASEY: You mean…a story.

HERNANDEZ: And you're in it.

CASEY: I'm in your story.

HERNANDEZ: As a witness.

CASEY: I'm not a witness to your story. I don't know
what the hell your story is. I couldn't figure it out in
Iraq; I sure as shit don't want to know about it now.

HERNANDEZ: Corroborating witness. Just have to tell
your own story. Which supports mine.

CASEY: And what is that story, Hernandez? You got
that figured out now?

HERNANDEZ: That there was a lack of leadership. That
he'd done this to other women. That he attacked me,
after you left. And that when you were there, Captain
Baines did the same to you.

CASEY: So you want me to fill out twenty forms and
write a story too.

(Pause)

HERNANDEZ: Basically. Yeah.

CASEY: Here's the story I heard was going around. I
think you know it. I think you were one of the prime
people keeping it going around. Nothing happened. It
was all in my head. I wanted a promotion and Baines
blocked it, I was hallucinating, I was on drugs, I was
bored, I was a slut, I was a crazy bitch so I made up a
story. Pick one of the above.

HERNANDEZ: We had our differences, Sergeant. I'm not
going to deny that. But I didn't know. I swear to God,
till after.

CASEY: You were not my friend.

HERNANDEZ: And I'm not proud of the way I treated you, among a few other things I'm not proud of. It got real crazy over there. Everything just spiraled out of control after—

CASEY: So, what is this, one of your steps on your twelve step journey?

HERNANDEZ: I understand your anger, believe me.

CASEY: I can't help you.

HERNANDEZ: Don't do it for me.

CASEY: Would I be doing myself a favor? Is that gonna make people like me any better? Is it gonna get rid of these fucking headaches, or my pounding heart, or the fact that I can't take a deep breath because my chest is so fucking tight.

HERNANDEZ: When you left, after all that shit went down with Kellerman—

CASEY: Stop right there. Kellerman was my fault and I'll be living with that the rest of my life, but I'm not gonna discuss that with you. You threw me under the bus.

HERNANDEZ: Just hear me out. Baines told Williams to always have me drive, even though he knew I was trained as a gunner. He did shit like that. Fucking mind games he played over there. I told you I was a gunner because I didn't want to drive. I was hoping you'd put me in the gun. And you did—.

CASEY: No. I woulda figured it out even if you didn't tell me. He was not good in the gun. I would've switched it around anyway. That was not your fault.

HERNANDEZ: They want us to be against each other. They set it up that way. Especially in Iraq. Maybe I didn't see it then, but I see it now. It works in their favor, if we stay that way. That's all I'm saying.

CASEY: Here's the thing Hernandez. You remember the advice you gave me on the side of MOBILE, my first mission out. About my little boy, you said put him in a box, throw away the key. I did that. Iraq is in that box now. I'm not opening that up for you.

HERNANDEZ: Then he gets away with it.

CASEY: He's gonna get away with it anyway.

HERNANDEZ: Maybe. Probably. But if you don't fight back, you're saying exactly what he's putting out there. That you wanted it. That you asked for it. That it was your fault. That you're a fuckin ho and deserved everything you got.

(CASEY *is stone cold silent.*)

HERNANDEZ: You do what you need to do, Sergeant. I'll get out of your hair now.

(*As* HERNANDEZ *exits out the door, lights alter.*)

(*The cell phone video footage and sounds of war start, we see humvees, trucks on a convoy from jerky, fragmented angles.*)

(BAINES *comes out of the closet. He puts his hand on her shoulder. He helps her into her flak jacket, puts on her kevlar helmet, and wipes a smear of blood on her cheek. The sound of loud ringing begins and continues throughout the following scene:*)

## Scene Twelve

(*Iraq. A staff meeting.* BAINES, HERNANDEZ *and* WILLIAMS *face* CASEY, *who is clearly in shock, ears ringing. We shouldn't be sure if this is real, a dream or something in between, but we experience it from her P O V.*)

BAINES: I asked you a question, Sergeant. Why were you behind the wheel of that humvee, Sergeant?

CASEY: Kellerman was rattled, sir. There were I E Ds everywhere. I decided it would be best if I drove, sir.

BAINES: Who was in the gun?

HERNANDEZ: Sergeant Johnson put me in the gun, sir.

CASEY: I didn't trust Kellerman in the gun. He's not able to pay attention, sir. I think he should have stayed back—

BAINES: He's staying back now because he's fucking dead. And whose fault is that, Sergeant? Lance Corporal? Staff Sergeant?

WILLIAMS: Sergeant Johnson understood, the team positions were set and were not to be changed, sir.

BAINES: Right from the start you have not stopped questioning the way things get done.

CASEY: I based my decision on what I believed was best for the sake of the mission—

BAINES: I have one question for you, Sergeant. Why did you swerve the Humvee to the right?

(CASEY *doesn't answer. The Shadow of* THE BOY *appears behind her.*)

BAINES: Somebody better fucking answer me.

HERNANDEZ: A local was standing in the middle of the road, sir. The boy ran between the tanks and the Humvee and was standing there when we approached. Sergeant Johnson swerved to miss him.

BAINES: A local.

CASEY: It was poor judgment on my part, sir.

BAINES: Poor judgment and a marine got his legs blown off.

(CASEY *doesn't answer; the ringing is drowning everything out.*)

BAINES: You should have kept that convoy moving, you should have plowed through little Haji like he was a skunk in the road. I'd rather have a thousand dead Baby Akmeds for even one dead Marine.

CASEY: It was—instinct, sir.

BAINES: Are you telling me your ovaries interfered with your decision making abilities on this mission? They send me a Walking Mattress and what do I get: another hole to plug.

CASEY: I'm having trouble hearing you, sir.

BAINES: Next time, you see a boy on the road playing chicken with a hundred vehicle convoy, you roll right over him.

CASEY: Yes sir.

BAINES: This debrief's over.

(As HERNANDEZ and WILLIAMS exit, to CASEY)

CASEY: Not you. Here.

(BAINES tosses CASEY a bottle of hand sanitizer, as she catches it:)

CASEY: BOOM! We all get a little blood on our hands. Use it. You got some blood right here.

(BAINES reaches out and wipes some blood off CASEY's face. He helps her out of her flak jacket, takes off the kevlar helmet. He pulls her hair out of her bun. BAINES tries to kiss her.)

CASEY: No! Stop! I'll—report you!

(BAINES pulls CASEY back, unzips his pants, she pushes him away, he yanks her back, forcing her down as she tries to fight him off.)

BAINES: You sure you want to open up that Pandora's Box, Sergeant Johnson?

CASEY: I'll file charges.

BAINES: Once you open it, you can't close it again, Sergeant.

*(As* BAINES *forces* CASEY *down again, standing behind her.)*

CASEY: Please….

BAINES: Now what good do you think is gonna come out of that?

*(*CASEY *fights, but* BAINES *is stronger. He yanks down her pants as lights black out.)*

## Scene Thirteen

*(*CASEY's *living room, Night. She bolts upright on the couch, her heart racing. Something startled her: a noise by the window? The room is dark except where there is a path of moonlight. A shadow passes the window. The window is opening. She grabs her gun from under the couch. A figure [*SEAN*] climbs into the window. It's the boy from Iraq. She thinks. Unable to think, she reacts, falls off the couch, backs into a corner of the room. She is breathing fast, tense, terrified. The figure stumbles over some things on its way to the door, and turns on the light revealing a ten year old curly headed, biracial boy. He sees her, freezes. She doesn't lower her gun right away; she's not sure what she's seeing.)*

SEAN: Mom, don't shoot me!

CASEY: Sean?

SEAN: You look different.

CASEY: What are you doing here? It's the middle of the night, what the hell time is it?

SEAN: I thought you were dead.

CASEY: Did somebody tell you that?

SEAN: No. I thought they were waiting…for a good time to tell me.

CASEY: People don't save bad news like that—

SEAN: I thought you had to be dead. You stopped writing. You stopped skyping.

CASEY: You didn't seem to want to talk to me Sean, I thought it would be easier if I—

SEAN: Why don't you want to see me, Mom?

CASEY: It's not that, Seanie.

SEAN: Dad said it's like the astronauts on the space shuttle. When they come back to earth they can't stand up because in space you're just floating around in zero gravity and your muscles shrink. The heart's a muscle. So it shrinks too. Their bodies have to learn how to be on earth again.

CASEY: I understand that.

SEAN: But you weren't in space. You were in Iraq, which has the same gravity as here.

CASEY: Sort of.

SEAN: In Call of Duty the avatars freeze after a bomb goes off near them. You have to wait for them to come back to life. Did that happen to you?

CASEY: Sean. It's the middle of the night, you really shouldn't've come here. I'm gonna haveta call Gramma.

SEAN: I want to stay here with you.

(CASEY is silent, panting.)

SEAN: Why can't I stay here? What's wrong with you?

CASEY: I'm not right yet, buddy. My heart is having trouble adjusting.

SEAN: I'm not your buddy!

CASEY: I'm not a good mother right now, Sean. Look. I can't take care of you. Not the right way—

SEAN: I could take care of you.

CASEY: It's not supposed to work that way, Bud. I know it's been hard. But I didn't want you to see me like this.

SEAN: I'm not a baby.

CASEY: Just a little longer.

SEAN: You missed my birthday! You missed all of fourth grade! How much longer do you need?

CASEY: I don't know.

SEAN: The fourth of July is next week. Dad said he didn't want to go downtown for the fireworks. He says they're too loud and sudden like rocket fire. I get it. But maybe you could take me to the French-fry park.

CASEY: Where?

SEAN: The French-fry park, up on the bluff by downtown, the park with the big yellow statue that looks like french-fries. We use to go on the fourth of July when I was little and afraid of the booms. You can see the fireworks, but you can't hear the sound. Can we go?

CASEY: I don't think I can…this year. Look Buddy—

SEAN: Stop calling me that! I'm not your buddy! A buddy doesn't treat another buddy like you did. Letting me think you were dead!

CASEY: I didn't know you thought that—

SEAN: You don't love me anymore.

CASEY: That's not it.

SEAN: "That's not it." You didn't say that's not true. Pause.

CASEY: You gotta go back to Grammas.

SEAN: Whhhyy???

CASEY: Oh my God. I'm not—Seanie, listen to what I'm trying to tell you. I shake, and I get dizzy and I have bad dreams, and I get headaches a lot, my nerves are shot, my heart is pounding for no reason, and I feel like I can't breathe and then I get real angry over stupid little things and I want to protect you from all of that. I didn't think it was fair to you—

SEAN: Well, this isn't fair either.

CASEY: No it's not. Life's not fair, Sean. You got that right. I'm calling Gramma.

SEAN: Gramma doesn't like to get woken up before she's ready. She doesn't have a lot of rules, but that's one of them. If you call her, she's not gonna be happy. Can't I just sleep in my room? Just 'til tomorrow. Just one night. Or I can sleep on the couch if you want.

CASEY: That's where I sleep.

SEAN: Then I can sleep in my room. I won't make any noise. I'll wake up early and make my bed in the morning and get my own breakfast and ride my bike back and be home before Gramma gets up. She won't even know I'm gone. I won't bother you. I promise.

CASEY: I need you to go back to Grammas, Sean.

SEAN: I wrote a report about you. I brought it with me, you wanna read it? I did a big poster too with pictures of you and other pictures I got from the Internet, about Iraq. It was for Heroes Week. I did you.

(SEAN *holds his report out to* CASEY, *she doesn't take it.*)

CASEY: I'm not a hero.

SEAN: What are you then?

CASEY: I'm…I'm tired. I'm…tired. I'm…sorry.

SEAN: Do you want to read my report?

CASEY: I can't right now.

SEAN: Can I just hug you then?

(SEAN *takes a step towards* CASEY *and the sound of a rifle shot rings out startling her. She freezes. As he moves towards her, a canyon still between them, the shadow of* THE BOY *appears.*)

SEAN: I wanted to hug you as soon as you got off the plane. I wanted to run up to you and hug you. Can I hug you now?

(*We hear the cell phone video:* Madonna! Madonna!*)*

SEAN: Mom? Mom?

(*Superimposed on* SEAN *is the cell phone video footage of* S'AHEED *shouting at her, arms reaching for candy. And then, before* CASEY *can open her arms,* SEAN *is running towards her. The cell phone video stops.* SEAN *hugs* CASEY. *At the same time* THE BOY *wraps his arms around her from the other side.* CASEY *reacts immediately throwing* SEAN *and* S'AHEED *away from her, in opposite directions.* THE BOY *disappears.*)

CASEY: Get away from me, goddamn you, don't you understand?! I can't take care of myself, how am I gonna take care of you?

(SEAN's *breath starts wheezing as he gets more agitated through the rest of the scene.*)

SEAN: I told you! I'll take care of you!

CASEY: No! Don't you get it? I don't care about you anymore!!

(SEAN *explodes into angry tears.*)

SEAN: Forget it then! I don't care about you either!!!

(SEAN *runs out the door.* CASEY *lets him go. If using video here as a transition we see: The cell phone video footage in fragments, images of Iraqi boys' faces shouting, bags of candy, humvees driving down highways, explosions, braying donkeys, the orange sky,* CASEY *skyping* SEAN, *a convoy approaching an overpass, a boy waving and shouting silently. We hear a female marine laugh, shout: "What's your name? Tell me your name?" We see the boy, the sky behind him, the road, the bridge. In the darkness we hear sound of a rifle shot. A pause. A second shot echoes.)*

*(Lights shift)*


## Scene Fourteen

*(The next morning.* KEVIN *uses his key and enters, slamming the door behind him. He walks right past* CASEY *to slam his fists on the table, he turns to face her. She is standing in the middle of the room, waiting for him, her body sensing danger, on high alert.)*

KEVIN: You draw your weapon and you point it at your son.

*(*CASEY *doesn't answer.)*

KEVIN: You let him ride his bike back to your mother's down a long dark road at two in the morning, having a frigging asthma attack.

*(*CASEY *doesn't answer.)*

KEVIN: You don't call me—you don't call your mother. You don't call anybody and tell us what just happened. Instead you sit here and open up another bottle working your way through your dead father's tequila. *(He slams the bottle into the trash.)* Tell me what is wrong with this picture, Casey!?

CASEY: Everything.

KEVIN: You got that right. Everything. So if you know all that, you did this because? Answer me!

*(*KEVIN *is moving at* CASEY, *maybe knocking a chair over. She stands up to him.)*

CASEY: Because fuck you!! I've had it with your holier than thou I-did-two-tours-and-I'm-all-right-but-I-will hold-your-hand-til-you-get-your-ass-to-the-VA bullshit! You're so understanding, you care about me; you got my back? I remember looking at your back walking out the door! So don't act like mister nice guy you care about me, you don't care about anybody but yourself, you never did!

KEVIN: I'm talking about Sean here. And you just crossed the line.

CASEY: You walked in the door with your P T S D and you didn't do squat with that boy unless you were fucking screaming at him because he spilled his goddamn cheerios. We had to walk on eggshells around you.

KEVIN: *(Overlapping)* Bullshit. P T S D. I didn't have no fucking P T S D. I came back from a war.

CASEY: And what did I come back from?

KEVIN: I'm not drawing a weapon on my kid. I never came close to hurting him.

CASEY: You get to be the by the book Marine, who keeps his shit together and tell everybody what's wrong with them with your fucked up analogies. Well, it's bullshit. You damaged him too.

KEVIN: I'm here now, Casey. And I'm going to do whatever I need to protect him.

CASEY: Here's what I know: when it was you who brought home the war, I had to get out of your way and shut the fuck up. We all had to be so understanding twenty-four/seven—

KEVIN: We're not talking about me. We're talking about what you did.

CASEY: You wanna talk 'bout me, let's do it. Let's talk about what it was like for me. I didn't have a friggin chance in that unit. It was not Christmas Eve talking about how we were gonna party when we got back and all the fun we were gonna have together. Nobody gave a shit about me, and when I was raped every single one of my "buddies" there turned a blind eye. Cause that's what it's like. And you know what I'm saying is true. Because you've done it. You can look me in the eye and say, damn Cakes that sucks what happened to you. But when it happened to some other Walking Mattress in your your platoon, did you stick up for her, did you back her up?

KEVIN: I don't know who you're talking about.

CASEY: Yeah, because she didn't mean anything! She was just an excuse to crack some jokes about some ho with your buddies.

KEVIN: None of this gives you license to point a loaded weapon at your child. I'm here for your weapon. Then we're going down to the base to report this. Three strikes, Marine. I'm not fooling around now.

(CASEY *pulls out the gun and aims it at* KEVIN.)

CASEY: Fuck no, you're not my C O.

KEVIN: Don't make me take it from you, Cakes.

CASEY: STOP CALLING ME THAT!

KEVIN: Fair enough. But you gotta give me your weapon now or I'm gonna take it from you.

(KEVIN *steps towards her. Simultaneously* BAINES *emerges out of the closet and takes a step towards her.* CASEY *fires her gun at* BAINES. KEVIN *wrestles the gun away from* CASEY. BAINES *watches as* CASEY *struggles against* KEVIN *in a rising panic with legs kicking, arms swinging, fighting back in a way she couldn't fight back against* BAINES *in Iraq.* KEVIN *gently, but firmly wraps his arms around her, bringing* CASEY *to the floor.* CASEY *screams at the image of* BAINES:)

CASEY: Get out! Get out of my house! Get out! Get out! Get out!!

KEVIN: *(Overlapping)* You're all right. You're all right. I got you. I got you. Calm down, you're all right.

(BAINES *exits.* CASEY *breaks down, for the first time, sobbing.)*

*(Lights fade to black)*

## Scene Fifteen

*(In the darkness we hear laughter. As lights rise, we see* HERNANDEZ *sitting at the kitchen table drinking a cup of coffee. She's laughing and relaxed.* CASEY'S *quiet, holding her mug.)*

CASEY: So what did you say?

HERNANDEZ: I didn't see anything that applied to me. So I drew a box. With a big black sharpie. Then in big letters: R-A-P-E. Check.

CASEY: What'd they say to that?

HERNANDEZ: They told me I didn't fill out their form right. Made me do it again. So I did it again: Big black letters: Another BOX, RAPE, CHECK.

CASEY: Bet they loved that.

HERNANDEZ: They gave me another form. I did it again. This time, they filed it, in the circular file. Yeah, then they started handing out the meds.

CASEY: *(Pulls out two fistfuls of pill bottles from a drawer, then even more)* Oh, I got a bunch of them too.

HERNANDEZ: One for anxiety—

CASEY: One for depression—

HERNANDEZ: One to help the one for depression—

CASEY: One for sleeping—

HERNANDEZ: One for I don't know what, waking up, I guess.

CASEY: One for my "old lady" bladder. This one must be for my "Personality Disorder".

HERNANDEZ: I love that one. They'd rather turn you into a Zombie than believe you.

(HERNANDEZ *takes the bottle* CASEY *is holding, and dumps the pills in trash.*)

HERNANDEZ: Forget this one. There's nothing wrong with your personality. There's something wrong with them.

CASEY: That means a lot coming from you.

HERNANDEZ: I wish I'd known you were so funny. We could have had some laughs on MOBILE.

CASEY: Yeah. That would've been a different story, huh?

HERNANDEZ: Yeah, I wish it was.

CASEY: *(Beat)* So I wrote one. A story. For both of us. I'm in.

HERNANDEZ: I appreciate that, Sergeant.

CASEY: Yeah.

*(Pause)*

HERNANDEZ: So. How's your little boy doing?

(CASEY *doesn't' answer, but* THE BOY *from Iraq is not there and neither is* BAINES. *A moment: two women drinking coffee in a kitchen in southwestern Pennsylvania. Then without warning* MARGIE *is in the doorway, wearing her Foodland smock ready for work.*)

MARGIE: I hate to bother you with this, Casey. But, I don't know where Kevin is. And I gotta be at work. I was late the last two times waiting for him. I can't be late again.

CASEY: So, what do you want from me? Call Kevin.

MARGIE: I called! He's not answering his cell phone. Why have a phone if you're not going to answer it? *(Sees* HERNANDEZ*)* Oh. I didn't know you had a friend—

CASEY: Oh, no, Mom this is Hernandez. I mean, this is Jamie Hernandez. This is, my Mother.

HERNANDEZ: Nice to meet you, Ma'am.

MARGIE: Well, I'm sorry to have to barge in like this but I'm kinda in a jam—

HERNANDEZ: No problem, I'll get out of your hair now. Thanks for the coffee. And—thank you. Let's keep in touch, Sergeant. *(She exits.)*

MARGIE: She seems nice.

CASEY: She's—she's okay. Where is he, Mom? Sean? Did you leave him at your house?

MARGIE: No. He's in the car. Can he come in, just for a little while? Till Kevin gets here.

CASEY: Can't you just bring him to Kevin's?

MARGIE: Casey, isn't it time to put this behind you? That's what they did. Every generation goes to war, after a time they put it behind them. Or they didn't. And then they turned out like your father. As much as I couldn't stand the sonovabitch, he was a tortured soul. I don't want to see you be like him.

*(*CASEY *doesn't answer.)*

MARGIE:  You seem lonely, Casey.

CASEY: Lonely is not the word I'd use.

MARGIE: Well, I'm proud of you.

CASEY: Oh god, don't be proud of me.

MARGIE: I am very proud. I still wear my button on my smock at work. And I tell everyone who will listen to me. How strong you are. They're not gonna beat you down. I know it. Not you.

CASEY: I'm glad you know it.

MARGIE: So can I leave him here?

*(No answer)*

MARGIE: You've been a great mother to that boy, from the moment he was born. You're not gonna be perfect all the time. You don't have to be. You don't even have to be good, not all the time.

*(KEVIN flies in. This is the first time CASEY's seen him since the last scene.)*

KEVIN: I'm here, I'm here, I'm here, don't worry, he's in my car, s'all good, you can go now, Margie. Sorry I was running late. But I'm here now.

MARGIE: Okay, thank God! I won't be home until after nine, so can he sleep at your place tonight?

KEVIN: No problem.

MARGIE: Okay, I gotta run. Did you need any of these refilled? I could drive you down to the V A tomorrow if you—

CASEY: No, I'll do it. I'm gonna drive down—myself. I'm gonna need the one for the headaches.

MARGIE: Okay, I'll call you later, Casey.

KEVIN: Hey Margie, tell him I'll be out in a minute.

*(MARGIE nods, exits. Long quiet between them)*

KEVIN: Cakes.

CASEY: Kev.

KEVIN: So.

CASEY: Yeah. *(Pause)* I went to the V A. That should make you happy. They're a bunch of asshats, but okay maybe it's better than holing up in here, slowly killing myself.

*(KEVIN nods. Pause)*

CASEY: I'm sorry for freakin out on you and shit. That was not good and I really don't know how to explain it, except, taking my weapon, leaves me with nothing—nothing to protect myself with, and I don't like that feeling. *(Beat)* And thank you. For not—going to the base. I don't know why you didn't. I would have. But it helps, that you didn't, so thank you. You keep the pistol. You better keep it. I could have shot you. I'm sorry, Kevin.

KEVIN: You're forgiven.

CASEY: What?

KEVIN: I said I forgive you. And I'm sorry. For everything. What happened to you. For what happened between us. For the way things are. For all that, I'm sorry.

CASEY: I filed charges. I'm in for it now.

KEVIN: You did what you needed to. Balls in their court now. No analogy will be made.

*(After a very brief pause)*

CASEY: I kept telling Sean: we're the good guys and they're the bad guys. We're fighting for freedom and democracy, we're saving them. We're doing noble things. Be proud. But I wasn't.

KEVIN: Good guys, bad guys, cowboys and Indians. It's not like that. What were we doing over there? We were serving our country, like we said we would, we took an oath, and we carried it out. Was I proud of

everything I did or didn't do over there? No. But look
at me. Cakes. This is the thing you gotta do. You gotta
start doing this right now.

CASEY: What?

KEVIN: Show yourself one quarter of the compassion I
know you'd show me if the situation was reversed. Be
kind to yourself.

(CASEY *doesn't know whether to laugh or cry.*)

CASEY: Okay, now I know you've been to a psycho-
terrorist!

(KEVIN *laughs.*)

CASEY: You're not denying it. "Be kind to yourself?"
The Kevin I know would say just get the fuck over it.

KEVIN: All right, give yourself a hug and a kiss and
then get the fuck over it. Then forgive yourself. And
that's all I got to say about the matter.

(KEVIN *begins to exit towards the door, going back to where*
SEAN *is waiting.*)

CASEY: *(Stated simply without emotion)* I shot a little boy.

(KEVIN *stops and turns to face* CASEY.)

CASEY: I thought he was about Sean's age, he was
probably older. He was in the village we always
passed soon after we'd leave the base. He'd wave, I'd
wave back. He'd yell for us to throw him candy, pens,
money, food. I started putting life savers in baggies
with pennies like it was Halloween and throw them
out to him when we rolled past. He started calling me
Madonna, I have no idea why. I asked him his name.
He was in the market and I asked him his name and
he smiled up at me, with this toothy grin, "S'aheed."
He was just this funny kid acting goofy on the side of
the road. Like Sean, he was a goofball. And I started
looking for him every time we passed. The others in

my unit knew him, said he was the son of an insurgent. Not to get friendly. They used them as decoys, to set you up for an ambush. Don't be fooled. They aren't normal kids. Don't think of them as kids. Think of them as the enemy. As soon as I got there, everything that could go wrong did. And then that last convoy, Kellerman was spooked, he really should've stayed back, he was driving erratic, he was gonna get us killed I thought, so I took over, I took the wheel and I started driving, Kellerman was on the radio. And the boy, S'aheed shows up in the road, he must've dodged in between vehicles at the last minute. There he is right in front of me. I swerve not to hit him, BOOM, there goes Kellerman. On the next mission, I saw the boy on an overpass. *(First time she pauses)* He had something in his hand, he was dropping it. I don't know what it was. Could have been a grenade. Could have been a rock. Could have been a snickers bar. I keep going over it in my head. When did I decide to lift my rifle, when did I aim, when did I pull the trigger. I don't remember thinking about it, or feeling one way or another about it. Took two shots. I missed the first time and then I hit the target. I aimed my weapon at a little boy and took him out. I was doing my job. The one time I didn't fuck it up in their opinion.

*(Pause.* KEVIN *doesn't push the moment.)*

CASEY: Maybe I deserved what happened to me.

KEVIN: *(Slow and deliberate)* No. Way.

CASEY: *(A brief pause)* Thank you, Kevin.

KEVIN: Semper fi.

CASEY: Semper fi.

*(*CASEY *breathes.* KEVIN *sees an opening.)*

KEVIN: There's somebody waiting for you outside. He's sitting in my car. I told him to wait there until I came out. Now I can leave and take him back to my place for dinner and then bed or I can text him and get him in here to say hi. *(Quick beat)* Yeah I got him a cell phone, we'll argue about that later. *(Quick beat)* We can go no further than that tonight. "Just hello, Mom, how you doin?" " I'm doin good, Seanie, how you doing?" *(Beat)* What do you say? Step by step. You tell me when you want to take the first step. *(Beat)* We're having fun and everything, but this single parenting is kicking my ass. I need you Cakes. He needs you.

(CASEY *stares at him for a minute, then without a word, she gets up, steps, walks, runs to the door. She opens the door and the room fills with light.)*

## END OF PLAY

www.ingramcontent.com/pod-product-compliance
Lightning Source LLC
Chambersburg PA
CBHW052210090426

42741CB00010B/2480